MAINE

A PICTURE MEMORY

Text
Bill Harris

Captions
Laura Potts

Design
Teddy Hartshorn

Photography
Colour Library Books Ltd.
FPG International

Picture Researcher
Leora Kahn

Commissioning Editor
Andrew Preston

Editorial
David Gibbon

Director of Production
Gerald Hughes

CLB 2857
© 1992 Colour Library Books Ltd, Godalming, Surrey, England.
All rights reserved.
This 1992 editon published by Crescent Books,
distributed by Outlet Books, Inc., a Random House Company,
40 Engelhard Avenue, Avenel, New Jersey 07001.
Color separations by Scantrans Pte Ltd, Singapore
Printed and bound in Singapore
ISBN 0 517 07269 6
8 7 6 5 4 3 2 1

MAINE

A PICTURE MEMORY

In an America crisscrossed by Interstates that pass shopping malls, chain motels and houses with all the charm of a pair of hundred-dollar sneakers, there is an almost universal urge to get away from it all, to get back to a time when the pace was slower and the people friendlier. The good news is that it is still possible. Just head north and east until you cross the border into Maine and your car can be transformed into a time machine that will take you back to the eighteenth century once you've turned off the beaten path. Yes, the eighteenth century. Those far-off days are alive and well all over the country and other parts of New England are proud of their mementoes of the Revolutionary War. But there are places in Maine that are still intact in their pre-Revolutionary condition, and people there whose way of life isn't a whole lot different from the daily routine common in colonial times.

Sure, Maine has turnpikes and toll booths and billboards advertising shopping centers that cater to bargain hunters. It has cute condos and seaside cottages at the end of roads trespassing on fragile wetlands in spite of the "no trespassing" signs. This is America, after all. But America's roots are still vigorous in the Pine Tree State and they are never far from the surface. The prevailing attitude among State O' Mainers is "if it ain't broke, don't fix it," and they are generally as capable of surviving without the help of outsiders as their great-grandfathers were, and many of them are working land or sailing waters that have been supporting their families for generations.

There are thousands of islands off the coast of Maine, and almost all of them have at least a trace of a house and a barn that once supported a family in a way that most of us have dreamed of recapturing at one time or another. But hundreds of them are still home to people who wouldn't trade their lives of isolation for any of the conveniences the rest of us consider the key to the good life. Most of them make their living from the water that surrounds them, and the majority of Maine people who are classified as fishermen go out at the crack of dawn each day in search of lobsters.

Chances are their grandfathers did the same work in the same way. Modern technology may have come in the form of plastic floats to replace the bottles and hand-carved pine buoys that were always used to mark the hand-made trap's location, and they may be attached with a length of nylon line rather than the traditional hemp, but lobstering is one of those industries that defies improvement. Some of them may have fiberglass boats and some may use manufactured traps, although they still call them pots, and none of them relies on oars to move through the water any longer, but the lobsterman's typical day hasn't changed in generations. The hard work begins at four in the morning, sailing through thick fog banks for as much as a hour looking for spots where the underwater ledges seem most likely to attract lobsters, and then dropping a baited trap overboard. In a day or two it will have to be hauled back on board, heavy with water and the flat stone that has held it in place and, hopefully, with an additional few pounds of live lobster. But the man who does the work is on his own and that's what makes it all worthwhile.

Of course, it's possible to go to the Farmer's Market in Portland and buy fresh vegetables proudly labeled "organically grown," and not far away from the house where Henry Wadsworth Longfellow grew up, the name Georgio Armani is likely to be more revered. But silk blouses and sun-dried tomatoes are just window-dressing to make visitors feel that Maine can be as sophisticated as Phoenix or Palm Beach. And if it encourages them to leave behind credit card slips with big numbers on them, it's a new tradition Down Easters can live with. Because, as they're reminded every time they look at a local license plate, the other name for the Pine Tree State is "Vacationland." Those visitors are worth $2 billion a year to the state's economy, compared to $124 million from commercial fishing.

Although they are basically friendly and neighborly, State O' Mainers have always resisted change in the way they live their lives and, of course, that's the key to their success as hosts. But it isn't as though they've just learned the art.

As far back as 1794, Jabez Ricker led the way when he began renting rooms to strangers up near Sebago Lake. His neighbors thought he was crazy, and they were sure of it when he started serving them meals, too. But people from Boston thought he had the right idea, and before long his house became a full-fledged hotel, which he named the Mansion House. His grandson,

Images of the Nesowadnehunk River (above and top left), Brassna Lake (left), and the west branch of the Penobscot River (below, bottom left, and facing page), show Maine at its most peaceful, and reveal something of its famed aura of solitude. Overleaf: Mount Katahdin, Maine's highest peak, in Baxter State Park.

Fall is the most spectacular of Maine's seasons. The foliage takes on a multitude of different colors, ranging from the brilliant yellows found at Ellis Creek (facing page top) and Ellis Falls (facing page bottom), to the beautiful coppery reds found at nearby Hanover (below) and in the Rangeley Lakes Region (top right). Vibrantly-colored leaves frame the church at Bethel (above) and lend character to the well-kept town of Rumford (bottom right). Right: Union Church in Mercer. Overleaf: fall colors reflected in the waters of the Androscoggin River.

Maine's capital, Augusta, lying in the west central region of the state, is home to the magnificent state capitol (below and facing page top). Facing page bottom: a peaceful scene at Lake Cobbosseecontee. Overleaf: the picturesque village of North Monmouth.

Facing page: Fort McClary, built in the early eighteenth century to defend the port city of Kittery. Hamilton House (above, below, right, and bottom right), situated on the Piscataqua River, near South Berwick, is one of southern Maine's architectural gems. Top right: Kennebunkport, the family home of President Bush. Overleaf: the Sayward-Wheeler House, York Harbor.

The construction of Portland Head Light (below), on Cape Elizabeth, was authorized by President Washington in 1791, to protect ships from southern Maine's rugged and treacherous coastline. The lighthouse overlooks Casco Bay and offers superb views of the bay and islands, such as Orrs Island (top right), that lie in its waters. Bottom right: South Freeport. Center right: Biddeford Pool, Saco Bay. Overleaf: Nubble Light – also known as Cape Neddick – facing the turbulent waters of the Atlantic.

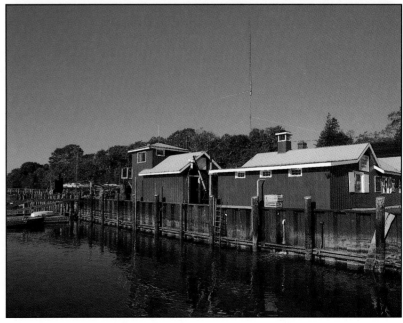

Portland (facing page) is Maine's largest and most populous city. Its harbor (facing page top) was the key to its early prosperity, and remains important today. The vicinity of Portland offers many attractions, including Portland Head Light (above) and Two Lights State Park (top left), as well as Orchard Beach (below), one of the most popular resorts on the coast. Left: the attractive town of Yarmouth. Bottom left: small craft moored off Bailey Island.

Friendship (below, top left, and bottom left), the original home of the Friendship Sloop – a dependable wooden sailboat common in the early twentieth century – is paradise for fishing and sailing enthusiasts alike. The pretty fishing village of Port Clyde (center left), situated at the tip of the peninsula that separates Muscongus and Penobscot bays, is well worth a detour. Overleaf: Rockland, the largest city in Maine's mid-coastal region, and the heart of its lobster industry.

Acadia National Park (these pages) was created in 1919 with lands donated to U.S. government and is the only national park in New England. The park, mostly situated on Mount Desert Island, is famed for its beauty and offers a variety of scenery ranging from the rocky coastline around Schooner Head (above), to long, beautiful beaches like Sand Beach (left), and marshland such as Bass Harbor Marsh (facing page top). Overleaf: a lake near Southwest Harbor.

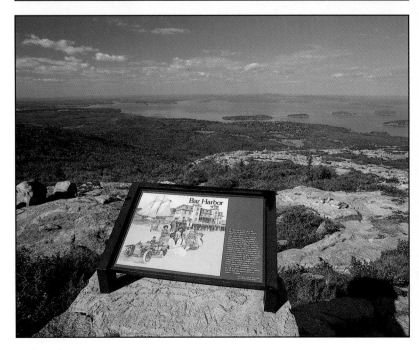

The streets of Bar Harbor (above), are crowded with visitors. The town, situated on Mount Desert Island, is the main gateway to Acadia National Park. A multitude of boats are moored in the blue waters of Northeast Harbor (facing page top), Bar Harbor (right), and Southwest Harbor (bottom right), in Acadia National Park. Top right: Beals Island. Below: lobster pots and colorful buoys. Overleaf: yachts and motor boats line a jetty in Northeast Harbor.

Below and facing page top: Bass Harbor Light, Mount Desert Island. Facing page bottom: boats silhouetted against a magnificent red sky in Sunset Harbor. Overleaf: Cutler Harbor. Following page: Quoddy Head Lighthouse, situated on the easternmost point in America.